Whose Fingerprints Are These?

Crime-Solving Science Projects

ROBERT GARDNER

Enslow Elementary

an imprint of

Enslow Publishers, Inc.

40 Industrial Road
Box 398
Berkeley Heights, NJ 07922
USA

http://www.enslow.com

Enslow Elementary, an imprint of Enslow Publishers, Inc.

Enslow Elementary© is a registered trademark of Enslow Publishers, Inc.

Library of Congress Cataloging-in-Publication Data

Whose fingerprints are these? : crime-solving science projects / Robert Gardner.
   p. cm. — (Who dunnit? Forensic science experiments)
Includes bibliographical references and index.
Summary: "Presents several forensic science experiments using fingerprinting techniques.
Includes science project ideas and crimes to solve"—Provided by publisher.
ISBN 978-0-7660-3245-3
1. Fingerprints—Juvenile literature. 2. Forensic sciences—Juvenile literature. 3. Forensic sciences—Experiments—Juvenile literature. 4. Science projects—Juvenile literature. I. Title.
HV6074.G37 2011
363.25'8—dc22

                      2008050065

Printed in the United States of America

102009 Lake Book Manufacturing, Inc., Melrose Park, IL

10 9 8 7 6 5 4 3 2 1

Illustration credits: © 2009 by Stephen Rountree (www.rountreegraphics.com)

Photo credits: AFP/Getty Images, p. 16; Jupiterimages, p. 18; © Mikael Karlsson/Alamy, p. 41; Shutterstock, pp. 1, 7, 15, 19, 26, 27, 29, 35, 36, 37, 45.

Cover photo: Shutterstock

Contents

Who Dunnit?
Forensic Science
Experiements

Introduction   p. 4
Entering a Science Fair   p. 4
The Scientific Method   p. 5
Safety First   p. 6

1 Fingerprints   p. 7

1-1   Your Fingerprints   p. 8

1-2   Making Fingerprint
      Records   p. 11

1-3   Who Dunnit?
      A Crime to Solve   p. 15

2 Latent Fingerprints   p. 19

2-1   Lifting Fingerprints   p. 20

2-2   Using Chemistry to See
      a Latent Fingerprint   p. 23

2-3   Who Dunnit?
      A Crime to Solve   p. 26

3 Lip Prints and Tooth Prints   p. 29

3-1   Lip Prints   p. 30

3-2   Tooth Prints   p. 33

3-3   Who Dunnit?
      A Crime to Solve   p. 35

4 Footprints and Other Tracks   p. 37

4-1   Looking for Tracks   p. 38

4-2   Footprint Evidence   p. 40

4-3   Who Dunnit?
      A Crime to Solve?   p. 42

Answers to Who Dunnit?
Crimes to Solve   p. 44

Words to Know   p. 46
Further Reading
  and Internet Addresses   p. 47
Index   p. 48

Experiments with a 🎗 symbol feature Ideas for a Science Fair Project.

Introduction

Crime scene . . . forensic evidence . . . fingerprints . . . DNA. You probably hear these words often. Forensic science television programs show scientists solving crimes. Perhaps you would like to try it, too. But what *is* forensic science?

Forensic science is used to solve crimes. The findings can be used in court. Scientists have to be very careful when they collect evidence. Evidence can put a person in jail. But some people have been found innocent and released from prison as a result of forensic evidence. In this book, you will learn about and practice some of the skills used by forensic detectives.

Entering a Science Fair

Some experiments in this book are marked with a 🎖 symbol. They are followed by ideas for a science fair project.

Judges at science fairs like experiments that are creative. So do not simply copy an experiment from this book. Expand on one of the suggested ideas. Or think up a project of your own.

The Scientific Method

Scientists try to understand how things work. They make careful observations. They do experiments to answer questions. Nearly all scientists use the scientific method. They: (1) observe a problem; (2) form a question; (3) make a hypothesis (a best-guess answer to the question); (4) design and do an experiment to see if the hypothesis is true; (5) analyze the results of the experiment; (6) if possible, form conclusions; (7) accept or reject the hypothesis. After their experiments, scientists share their findings. They write articles telling other scientists about their experiments and results.

How do you begin a project you can use in a science fair? You start by noticing something that makes you curious. So you ask a question. Your question might arise from an earlier experiment, something you saw, something you read, or for another reason.

Once you have a question, you can make a hypothesis—a possible answer to the question. Then you can design an experiment. The experiment will test your hypothesis. For example, suppose your question is "Do fingerprints fade away in sunlight?" You would place one set of prints in the sun, and one set in the dark. Both sets should be kept at the same temperature, be made on the same surface, and so forth. Sunlight will be the only difference between the two groups.

During the experiment, you would collect data by observing the prints. Does either set of prints start to fade? Does either set begin to change in any other way? You might take photographs of the prints every day. You would compare the data collected from the two sets over a few days. You might then be able to make a conclusion.

Your experiment might lead to other questions. These questions will need new experiments. That's the nature of science!

Safety First

To do experiments safely always follow these rules:

1 Always do experiments under **adult** supervision.

2 Read all instructions carefully. If you have questions, check with the adult.

3 Be serious while experimenting. Fooling around can be dangerous to you and to others.

4 Keep your work area clean and organized. When you have finished, clean up and put materials away.

Fingerprints

Edmond Locard (1877–1966) was a French forensic scientist. He said that every criminal leaves something behind and carries something away from a crime. The things left behind or carried away become the evidence used to solve the crime.

Criminals often leave fingerprints at a crime scene. Fingerprints are important evidence. Why? Because no two people have the exact same prints. Even identical twins have different fingerprints. In this chapter, you will start to learn about how scientists use fingerprints to solve crimes.

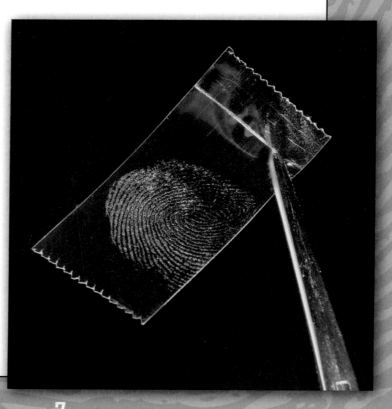

🎗 1-1 Your Fingerprints

1 Turn your hand so you see your palm. Look at the ends of your fingers and thumb (Figure 1a). You will see a pattern of curved lines. A magnifying glass will help you to see them more clearly. These lines are raised ridges of skin. They contain tiny openings (pores) connected to sweat glands in your skin. These ridges help you grip objects. If your fingertips were perfectly smooth, objects would slip from your fingers.

THINGS YOU WILL NEED:
- magnifying glass (convex lens)
- several people

These ridges have three basic patterns—arch, loop, and whorl (Figure 1b) Sometimes you will see a combination of patterns, like a whorl in an arch (Figure 1c).

2 Look carefully at the fingerprints on each of your fingers and thumbs. Do they all have the same pattern? How many fingers have an arch pattern? How many have a loop pattern? A whorl pattern? A combination of patterns?

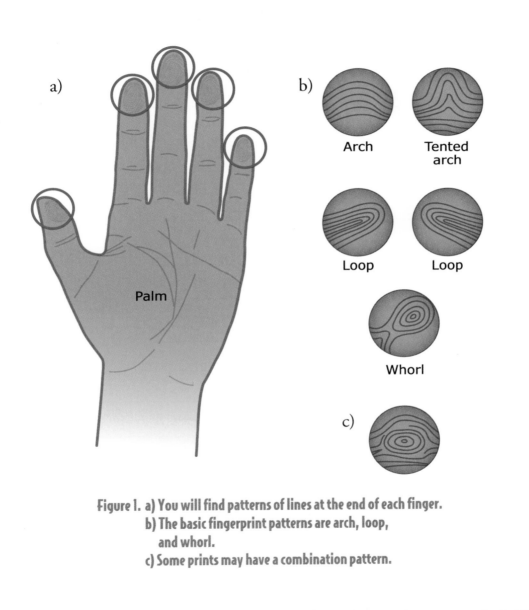

Figure 1. a) You will find patterns of lines at the end of each finger.
b) The basic fingerprint patterns are arch, loop, and whorl.
c) Some prints may have a combination pattern.

3 Look more carefully. Fingerprints have lots of details. Some of those details are shown in Figure 2. How many details can you find in the lines on your fingers?

4 Use a magnifying glass to look at other people's fingerprints. How do they differ from yours?

Ending Ridge	
Fork	
Short Ridge	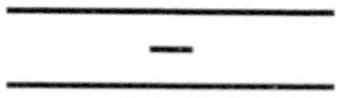
Dot	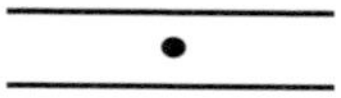
Bridge	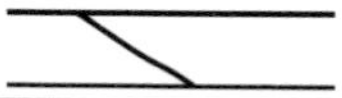
Hook	
Eye	
Double Fork	
Delta	
Triple Fork	

Figure 2. Details found in fingerprints make each print unique.

🎗 1-2 Making Fingerprint Records

1 Recording fingerprints with ink can be messy. You can record fingerprints in a different way. Use a sharp pencil with soft lead. Rub the pencil on a sheet of paper. Spread a heavy layer of graphite (pencil lead) on the paper. (See Figure 3a.)

2 Push the end of your right index finger onto the sheet of paper. Rub that fingertip in the graphite (Figure 3b). Push down hard. The end of your finger should become thoroughly coated with graphite.

THINGS YOU WILL NEED:

- sharp pencil with soft lead (#2 HB)
- paper
- several people
- wide, clear tape (3/4-inch wide or more)
- index card (3 inch x 5 inch)
- large card (5 inch x 8 inch) (optional)

Figure 3.
a) Use a pencil with very soft lead (graphite) to spread a heavy layer of graphite on a piece of white paper.

b) Rub the end of your right index finger in the graphite.

a)

b)

11

3 Have a partner remove a length of wide, clear tape. He should be careful to touch only the ends of the tape.

4 Your partner should place the center of the tape firmly on your coated fingertip (Figure 4a). He should then remove the tape and stick it on a 3-inch x 5-inch index card (Figure 4b).

5 Examine the tape on the card. It is a fingerprint record of your right index finger. Write your name and "right index finger" under the fingerprint.

Figure 4.
a) Remove the fingerprint with clear, wide, plastic tape.

b) Place the tape carrying the fingerprint on an index card.

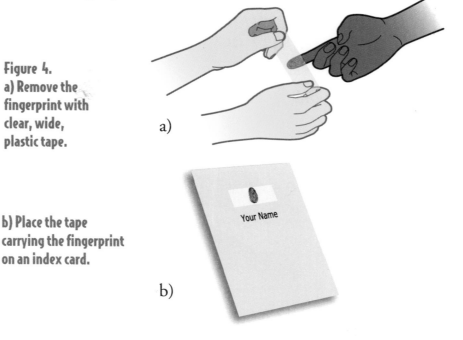

a)

Your Name

b)

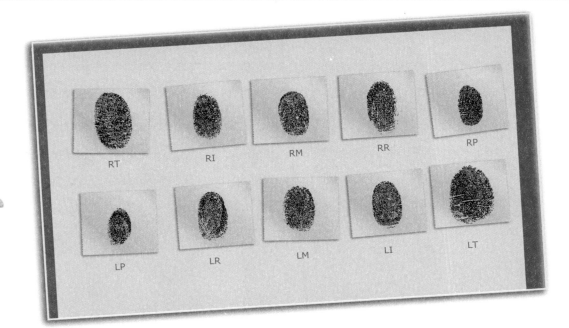

Figure 5. A complete set of fingerprints can be taped to a large card and labeled. R = right; L = left; T = thumb; I = index finger; M = middle finger; R = ring finger; P = pinkie.

6 If you wish, you and your partner can do this for each of your fingers. (It isn't necessary.) The fingerprints can be taped to a 5-inch x 8-inch file card or a sheet of paper. (See Figure 5.) In later experiments we will use only the fingerprints of right index fingers. Doing each finger can take a lot of time.

7 Now record the fingerprint of your partner's right index finger. If you wish, you can record all his fingerprints.

8 Record the fingerprints of the right index finger of several people. They might be members of your family, classmates, or friends. Be sure to record each person's name under his or her fingerprint.

Ideas for a Science Fair Project

• Record fingerprints by pressing a person's finger against an ink pad. Then roll the finger across a file card. Compare these records with those made using graphite and clear tape. Which method do you prefer?

• Figure out other ways to record fingerprints.

• Collect at least 100 fingerprints. What percentage are arch type? Loop type? Whorl type? A combination of types?

• Do toes have toe prints? If so, do they have the same patterns—arches, loops, and whorls?

Who Dunnit? A Crime to Solve

You are called to the scene of a robbery. You discover a dirty fingerprint of an index finger (right). It is on a door frame—the door the robber pried open to enter the home. You photograph the fingerprint. It does not match the fingerprints of anyone who lives there. You conclude it was left by the robber.

Your police department has fingerprints of previously convicted robbers on file. Four of those people are no longer in prison. Their index finger fingerprints are made available to you. Their names are listed below their fingerprints.

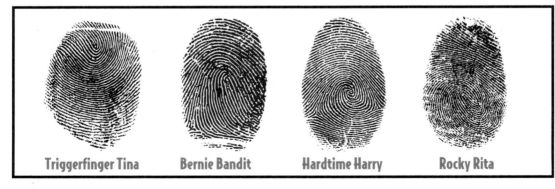

| Triggerfinger Tina | Bernie Bandit | Hardtime Harry | Rocky Rita |

Examine the fingerprints. Which have arches? Loops? Whorls? Combinations? What do you conclude? Who would you bring in for questioning?

Fingerprint Facts

When police record fingerprints, they use ink. They roll a person's finger on an ink pad. Then they roll the finger on a card. They do this for each finger and thumb. After the ink dries, they have a permanent record of a person's fingerprints. The card also has other information about the person, such as his or her  name, date of birth, place of birth, height, eye color, gender, and so on. Fingerprints may also be recorded electronically. A scanner transfers the fingerprints to a computer database.

Another Crime to Solve

1 Bring together people whose fingerprints you recorded in Experiment 1-2. Tell them that you are going to leave the room. Ask that one of them pretend to be a criminal. The "criminal" should leave fingerprints on a sheet of paper. You will not know which person made the prints.

2 The "criminal" should place his right index finger gently on a stamp pad. He should use that finger to leave two fingerprints on a sheet of white paper. One print will be darker than the other.

3 After they leave, return to the room. Examine the two fingerprints left at the "crime scene."

4 Compare the prints with those you recorded in Experiment 1-2. Can you identify a "suspect?" The prints will be mirror images of the ones you recorded. Therefore, you may want to hold the suspect's prints over a small mirror.

Father of Forensics

Edmond Locard, the "father of forensic science," was asked to investigate a series of robberies in a French city. He examined fingerprints taken from windows of homes that had been robbed. The fingerprints resembled human fingerprints. But Locard could tell that they were not human. He believed they were those of a monkey.

In those days (the early 1900s), organ-grinders were common on city streets. They were street musicians. Organ-grinders often had a pet monkey. The monkey would hold a cup and accept money from people passing by. Locard had police bring the local organ-grinders and their monkeys to headquarters. All the monkeys were fingerprinted. Locard examined the prints and quickly identified the thief.

The monkey's owner had taught him to enter second-story bedrooms and steal small, shiny objects or jewelry. The organ-grinder would then sell the stolen jewelry. He was arrested and his monkey was sent to the local zoo.

Latent Fingerprints

Often, there are fingerprints at a crime scene that cannot be seen. Such fingerprints are called latent fingerprints. (*Latent* is from the Latin word *latens*, to be hidden.) Forensic scientists look for surfaces where fingerprints are likely to be found. They spray these surfaces with a purple liquid, such as ninhydrin. The ninhydrin sticks to the chemicals in the fingerprints and becomes purplish. After a few hours, any latent fingerprints will become visible. The fingerprints can then be photographed or lifted (removed). To lift a fingerprint, the print is dusted (covered with a fine powder). Then clear tape is placed on the print. The powder used to dust the print will stick to the tape. When the tape is removed, the fingerprint will be on the tape. The lifted fingerprints can be taken to a crime lab for analysis.

🎗 2-1 Lifting Fingerprints

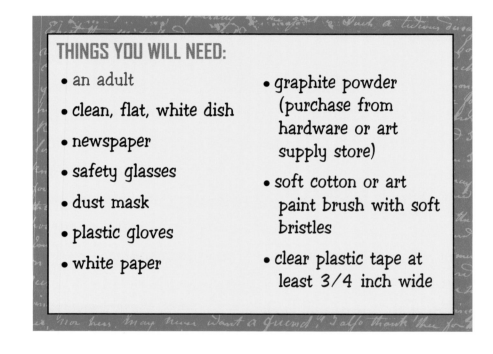

THINGS YOU WILL NEED:

- an adult
- clean, flat, white dish
- newspaper
- safety glasses
- dust mask
- plastic gloves
- white paper
- graphite powder (purchase from hardware or art supply store)
- soft cotton or art paint brush with soft bristles
- clear plastic tape at least 3/4 inch wide

Do this experiment under close adult supervision. You will be using powdered graphite. You should not breathe in any of the powder. Wear a dust mask.

Forensic scientists may use powder to lift fingerprints at a crime scene. You can lift a fingerprint in the same way.

1 Place a clean, flat, white dish on a newspaper.

2 Rub your right index finger along the side of your nose or your forehead. Then press the same finger against the center of the white dish (Figure 6a). Turn the dish in different ways. You may be able to see the print.

3 Put on safety glasses, a dust mask, and plastic gloves.

4 Carefully add a small amount of graphite powder near, not on, the fingerprint.

5 Dip a small piece of soft cotton into the graphite. You can also use a clean art paint brush with soft bristles. Use the cotton or brush to spread graphite lightly over the fingerprint (Figure 6b). Spread the graphite in all directions over the fingerprint. This will allow the graphite to stick to as many ridges as possible.

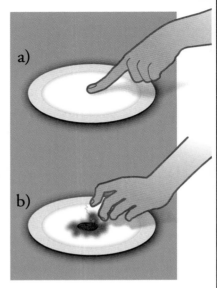

**Figure 6. a) Make a fingerprint on a white dish.
b) Dust the fingerprint. Use soft cotton to spread graphite over the print.**

6 Place a length of clear, wide, plastic tape on the fingerprint you dusted with graphite (Figure 7a). Be sure you do not touch the part of the tape used to cover the print. Smooth the tape against the print.

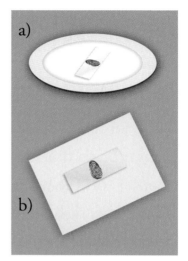

Figure 7. a) Lift the print with wide, clear, plastic tape.
b) Place the tape with the fingerprint on a piece of white paper.

7 Carefully remove the tape. You have lifted a fingerprint. Put the tape on a sheet of white paper (Figure 7b). You should have a fingerprint you can see clearly. If not, repeat the process. Lifting fingerprints is not easy. Even forensic scientists often fail to lift a complete fingerprint. You may need to practice the lifting process.

8 Compare the lifted fingerprint with your fingerprint record—the one you made in Experiment 1-2. Are the patterns the same?

Idea for a Science Fair Project

• Collect fingerprints and toe prints from a friend or a family member. Do toe prints and fingerprints match?

🎗 2-2 Using Chemistry to See a Latent Fingerprint

An adult must help you with this experiment.
Forensic scientists sometimes use chemicals
to see latent fingerprints. In this experiment
you will use cyanoacrylate, a chemical in
superglue, to see a latent fingerprint.

THINGS YOU WILL NEED:
- an adult
- well-ventilated area
- small plastic box such as the kind toothpicks sometimes come in. The box must be one you can seal
- aluminum foil
- clear tape
- your fingerprint from Experiment 1-2
- superglue

1 Find a small plastic box with a lid. The box should be one you can seal.

2 Rub your right index finger along the side of your nose or your forehead. Use that finger to make a fingerprint on a small piece of aluminum foil (Figure 8a). Once the print is made, be careful not to touch that part of the aluminum foil.

3 Tape the foil to the inside of the plastic box's lid (Figure 8b). The side of the foil with the fingerprint should be facing the superglue beneath it.

4 Fold another piece of aluminum foil to make a small pan. Put the pan on the bottom of the box **in a well-ventilated area.**

5 **Ask an adult** to squeeze about 20 drops of superglue into the little pan. **Warn the adult! Don't get superglue on your fingers.** It sticks to everything it touches!

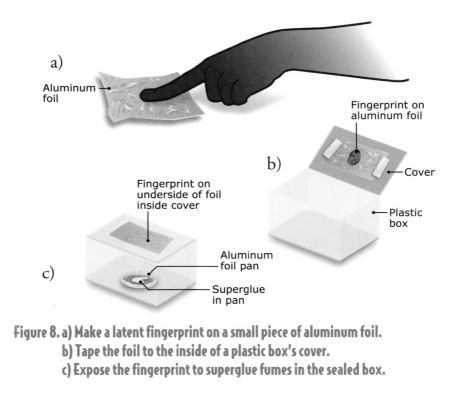

a)

Aluminum foil

Fingerprint on aluminum foil

b)

Cover

Fingerprint on underside of foil inside cover

Plastic box

Aluminum foil pan

c)

Superglue in pan

Figure 8. a) Make a latent fingerprint on a small piece of aluminum foil.
b) Tape the foil to the inside of a plastic box's cover.
c) Expose the fingerprint to superglue fumes in the sealed box.

6 Seal the box with clear tape (Figure 8c). The cyanoacrylate fumes will slowly collect on the body oils in the fingerprint. Allow four to five hours for a grayish-white print to develop.

7 Open the box. Examine the aluminum foil taped to the box's top. You should see a fingerprint.

8 Compare the fingerprint with a record of your fingerprint—the one you made in Experiment 1-2. Are the patterns the same?

9 **Ask an adult** to wrap any remaining superglue in aluminum foil and put it in a trash can.

Ideas for a Science Fair Project

• Make latent fingerprints on different surfaces. You might try paper, metal, cloth, wood, and others. From which surfaces can you lift fingerprints easily? From which surfaces is it difficult to lift fingerprints? Do this **under adult supervision**. Do not breathe in powdered graphite. Wear a dust mask and plastic gloves.

• Examine the paws of a dog or cat. Do these animals' paw prints resemble fingerprints?

Who Dunnit? A Crime to Solve

You are called to the scene of a robbery. You discover a thumbprint (left) on the glass sliding door where the robber entered. You use a piece of tape to lift the print. It does not match the thumbprints of anyone who lives in the home. You conclude it was left by the robber.

The local police department provides thumb prints of four burglary suspects. The thumb prints of the suspects are shown on below.

Next to each print is the name of the person from whom the thumb print was taken. What do you conclude? Who would you bring in for questioning?

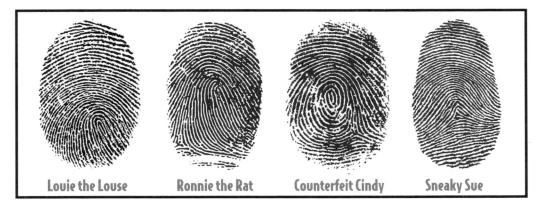

| Louie the Louse | Ronnie the Rat | Counterfeit Cindy | Sneaky Sue |

Create Your Own Crime to Solve

1 Gather the people whose fingerprints you recorded in Experiment 1-2. Tell them that after you leave the room you would like one of them to pretend to be a "criminal." They should not tell you who the criminal is.

2 Leave the room. The criminal should rub his (or her) right index finger along his forehead. That finger should then be pressed against a window in the room.

3 Have the criminal repeat step 2 and leave a second fingerprint on the window.

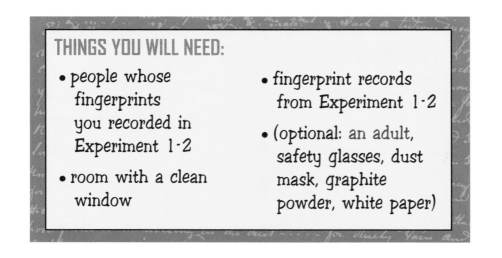

THINGS YOU WILL NEED:

- people whose fingerprints you recorded in Experiment 1-2

- room with a clean window

- fingerprint records from Experiment 1-2

- (optional: an adult, safety glasses, dust mask, graphite powder, white paper)

4 After several minutes, return to the room. Pretend there was a robbery. Look for the "robber's" fingerprints on a window.

5 Compare the fingerprints with the ones you have on record. Can you identify the "robber"?

6 If not, put a piece of clear wide plastic tape on one of the fingerprints and lift it. Can you identify the print now? If not, **put on safety glasses, a dust mask, and plastic gloves. Under adult supervision,** dust the second print with graphite powder. Lift that print.

7 Put the print on white paper. Use your fingerprint records to identify the criminal.

John Dillinger was a notorious criminal. He used acid to remove the skin from his fingertips. Police later found that his new fingerprints were identical to his old ones. His fingerprints had grown back.

Lip Prints and Tooth Prints

As you have seen, fingers leave prints. They can be visible or invisible. Other parts of your body may also leave prints.

You have probably seen lip prints on a drinking glass. Women who wear lipstick often leave their lip prints on a cup or glass. After eating chocolate or ice cream, you may have left your lip prints on a glass.

More than one crime has been solved by bite marks. Killers sometimes bite their victims. And victims sometimes bite their attacker. Forensic dentists are often able to use tooth prints or bite marks to identify a criminal.

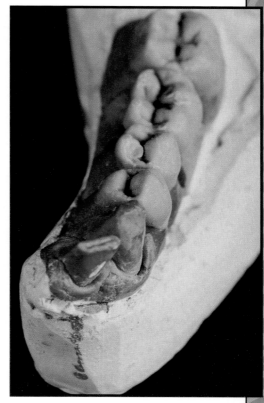

🎗 3-1 Lip Prints

It is easy to make lip prints.

1 Put some bright lipstick on your lips. Rub your lips together. This will spread the color evenly across your lips.

THINGS YOU WILL NEED:
- bright lipstick
- white paper or tissue
- magnifying glass
- people from whom you can collect lip prints
- pen
- clear tape
- drinking glass

2 Fold a sheet of white paper or tissue in half. Put the paper or tissue between your lips and press your lips together. Don't press hard. You might smudge the print. Examine the print with a magnifying glass.

Figure 9 shows some common lip prints. Some people may have a combination of lip print patterns. What lip print pattern or combination do you see in your lip prints?

3 Collect lip prints from as many people as possible. You might collect lip prints from family members, friends, or classmates. Label each print with the name of the person who made it.

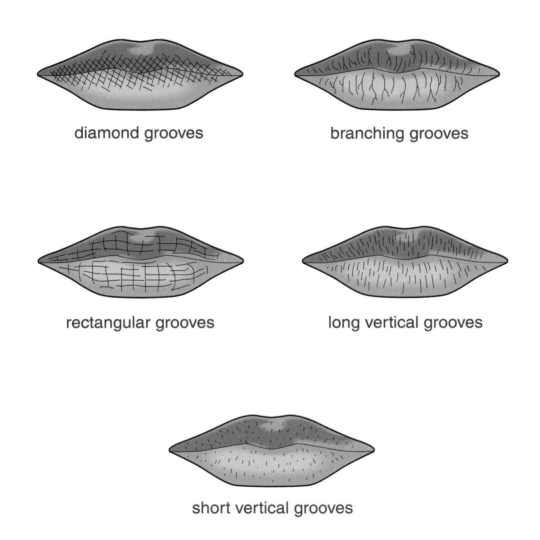

diamond grooves

branching grooves

rectangular grooves

long vertical grooves

short vertical grooves

Figure 9. Some common lip print patterns are shown.

4 Gather a group of people whose lip prints you have recorded. Ask them to have one person pretend to be a "criminal." The "criminal" should leave his or her lip prints on a glass after you leave.

5 After a few minutes, return to the "crime scene." Examine the lip print with a magnifying glass. Compare what you find with the lip prints you have recorded. Can you identify the "criminal" who left the lip print?

6 Do you think you can use clear tape to remove a lip print left on a drinking glass? Try it. Were you successful?

Ideas for a Science Fair Project

• Collect a large number of lip prints. Do any two people have the same lip print pattern? Do you think lip prints could be used to identify a suspect?

• Collect lip prints from members of different families. Try to collect lip prints from as many families as possible. Does heredity seem to play a role in lip print patterns?

3-2 Tooth Prints

1 Use scissors to cut squares from several clean Styrofoam cups. The squares should be about 8 centimeters (3 inches) on all sides.

2 Put two Styrofoam squares, one on top of the other, into your mouth. Bite down firmly on the Styrofoam. Remove them from your mouth.

3 Label the top piece "Upper" and the bottom piece "Lower." Compare the tooth print impressions. What differences do you see between upper and lower tooth prints?

4 Collect tooth print impressions from family members, friends, or classmates. Label the top and bottom teeth marks and the name of the person who made them.

5 Gather a group of people whose tooth prints you have recorded. Ask them to have one person pretend to be a

"criminal." The "criminal" should leave his or her tooth prints on a piece of cheese after you leave.

6 After a few minutes, return to the "crime scene." Examine the cheese with a magnifying glass. Compare what you find with the tooth prints you have recorded. Can you identify the "criminal" who bit the cheese?

Tooth prints have been used to solve real crimes. In one case, detectives found a wad of chewing gum at the scene of a murder. The stale gum had hardened. It had tooth marks in it. A forensic dentist made casts of the impressions in the hardened gum. The teeth that chewed the gum did not match the victim's teeth. But they did match teeth impressions made by a suspect. Forensic scientists were also able to collect some saliva from the gum. By testing the saliva, they found it was from a person with type AB blood. Type AB blood is found in only four percent of the population. The suspect had type AB blood. Facing both pieces of evidence, the suspect confessed to the murder.

Who Dunnit? A Crime to Solve

A house was robbed. You are asked to investigate the crime. You see that someone has removed cherry candy from a box on the kitchen counter. You discover a glass by the sink. There are dark lip prints on the glass. Perhaps the robber ate the red candy and then drank water.

The people who live in the house tell you they had not opened the box of candy. You conclude the robber left the lip prints. You ask local police officers to help. They question three suspects who

Suspect 1

Suspect 2

Suspect 3

were seen near the house that was robbed. You collect lip prints from each suspect. You compare their lip prints with the ones on the glass. What do you conclude? What additional evidence would you look for?

Footprints and Other Tracks

Criminals may avoid leaving fingerprints by wearing gloves. But they often leave other "prints." Their cars may leave tire tracks on driveways, lawns, or pavement. Such tracks may match the tires on their cars. Criminals can't fly. As a result, they may leave footprints that match shoes in their closets. Shoe tracks may be seen in snow, on muddy or soft dirt, on slushy sidewalks, or on dusty floors. Soil, dust, and stones may stick to their shoes or tires. Forensic scientists may trace such evidence back to the crime scene.

🎗 4-1 Looking for Tracks

THINGS YOU WILL NEED:

• access to outdoor and indoor places where tracks might be found

1 Go on a track hunt. You will find lots of tracks in light snow, soft or muddy soil, loose dirt, damp pavement, dusty floors, and other places.

2 Can you identify the tracks? Were they made by humans? Animals? Cars or trucks? Raindrops? Other things?

3 Look for tire tracks. Were they made by a car? A truck? A bicycle? Something else?

4 Look for human tracks. Were they made by a man? A woman? A child? How can you tell?

5 Estimate the shoe sizes of the people who made the tracks.

6 Figure 10 shows tracks made by a number of different animals. Dog, cat, and bird tracks are probably the ones you see most often. How many tracks of different animals can you find around your home? What animals made them?

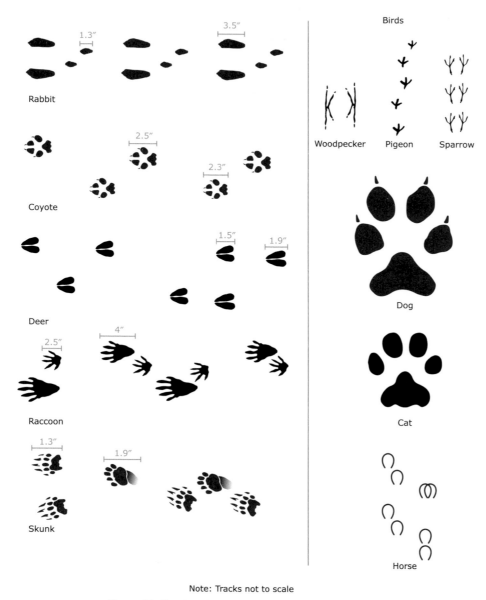

Birds

Rabbit — 1.3″ — 3.5″

Woodpecker Pigeon Sparrow

Coyote — 2.5″ — 2.3″

Dog

Deer — 1.5″ — 1.9″

Cat

Raccoon — 2.5″ — 4″

Skunk — 1.3″ — 1.9″

Horse

Note: Tracks not to scale

Figure 10. Tracks of some common animals are shown.

🎗 4-2 Footprint Evidence

1 Pour a thin layer of moist soil or fine beach sand into a cardboard box that is at least 12 inches long.

2 Gather a group of people—family, classmates, or friends. Ask that one of them pretend to be a "criminal." After you leave the room, the "criminal" is to step into the box and leave a shoe print in the soil or sand. The "criminal" will then brush off his or her shoe before you return.

3 When you return, examine the footprint. Was it made by a right or a left foot? Do you think it was made by a man? A woman? A boy? A girl?

4 Examine the bottoms of the shoes of the group you gathered together. Compare the shoes with the footprint. Can you identify the "criminal"?

THINGS YOU WILL NEED:

- moist soil or fine beach sand
- cardboard box that is at least 12 inches long
- several people
- hand brush
- ruler

Idea for a Science Fair Project

Use plaster of Paris to make a paste. Use the paste to make a cast of a footprint. You might make an exhibit of casts of different animal footprints.

Footprints and tire marks left in soft soil can be moved to the crime lab. There they can be compared with known makes of tires and shoes. To move a footprint or tire mark, plaster of Paris or dental stone is used. The pasty material is poured into the impression and allowed to harden. The cast can then be moved to a crime lab for further study.

Who Dunnit? A Crime to Solve

A neighborhood family is concerned. They put their garbage and trash barrels out on Monday evening. The waste disposal truck came early the next morning. When the family went out to bring the barrels back in, there was trash and garbage all over the sidewalk. They complained to the waste disposal company. The company told them that the barrels had been turned over when they arrived at sunrise. You are asked to investigate on Tuesday morning.

Overnight on Monday, a light snow had fallen. You hurry to examine the "crime scene." You observe the footprints seen in Figure 11. You tell the family you have solved the "crime." What do you tell them?

Figure 11. The crime scene

Answers to Who Dunnit?
Crimes to Solve

1-3: Hardtime Harry's fingerprint matches the one found at the crime scene. He should be brought in for questioning.

2-3: Sneaky Sue's fingerprint matches the one found at the crime scene. She should be called in for questioning.

3-3: The lip print of suspect 1 matches the print found on the glass. That suspect should be taken in for questioning.

4-3: You notice three types of footprints in the snow: bird footprints, human footprints, and raccoon footprints. You know birds are not strong enough to knock over a trash can, so it must have been a human or a raccoon. Since the human footprints appear on top of some of the raccoon prints, the raccoon was there before the people.

This is added proof that the raccoon knocked over the trash before the waste disposal company arrived. He probably turned over the trash cans while searching for food. His footprints gave him away.

Words to Know

bite marks (tooth prints)—The marks left by teeth in food or the flesh of some crime victims.

cyanoacrylate—The chemical in superglue. It is used to make latent fingerprints visible.

evidence—The things left behind or carried away from a crime scene. These things can be used to solve crimes and to convict criminals in a court of law.

fingerprints—The pattern of skin ridges found on the palm sides of fingers and thumbs. No two people have the same pattern.

footprints—Patterns left by the feet of humans and animals.

forensic science—The science used to investigate and solve crimes. It is also used in courts of law.

latent fingerprints—Fingerprints that are not visible.

lifting fingerprints—Removing fingerprints from a surface.

lip prints—Patterns left by lips when in contact with drinking glasses or other surfaces.

ninhydrin—A chemical solution sprayed on latent fingerprints to make them visible.

Further Reading

Bardhan-Quallen, Sudipta. *Championship Science Fair Projects: 100 Sure-To-Win Experiments*. New York: Sterling Publishing, 2004.

Bochinski, Julianne Blair. *The Complete Workbook for Science Fair Projects*. New York: John Wiley and Sons, 2005.

Fridell, Ron. *Forensic Science*. Minneapolis: Lerner Publications Company, 2007.

Hopping, Lorraine Jean. *Crime Scene Science: Investigating a Crime Scene*. Milwaukee: World Almanac Library, 2007.

Rhadigan, Joe, and Rain Newcomb. *Prize-Winning Science Fair Projects for Curious Kids*. New York: Lark Books, 2004.

Internet Addresses

Access Excellence: The Mystery Spot
<http://www.accessexcellence.org/AE/mspot/>

F.B.I. Youth
<http://www.fbi.gov/kids/6th12th/6th12th.htm>

Who Dunnit?
<http://www.cyberbee.com/whodunnit/crime.html>

Index

A

animal tracks, 39

arches, 8, 9

B

bite marks, 29, 33–34

C

chewing gum, 34

crime-solving activities
    fingerprints, 15–17,
        26–28
    footprints, 42–43
    lip prints, 32,
        35–36
    tooth prints, 33–34

cyanoacrylate, 23

D

Dillinger, John, 28

E

evidence, 4, 7,
    34, 37

experiments,
    designing, 5–6

F

fingerprints
    details, 10
    identical twins, 7
    latent, 19, 23–25
    lifting, 20–22
    overview, 7
    patterns, 8–9
    recording, 11–14,
        16
    removing, 28

footprints
    casts, 40–41
    identifying, 38–39
    overview, 37

forensic science, 4

I

impressions,
    making, 33

L

latent fingerprints,
    19, 23–25

lip prints, 29–32,
    35–36

Locard, Edmond,
    7, 18

loops, 8, 9

N

ninhydrin, 19

O

organ-grinders, 18

S

safety, 6, 20

saliva, 34

science fairs, 4

scientific method, 5–6

T

tented arch, 9

tire tracks, 37, 41

tooth prints, 29,
    33–34

W

whorls, 8, 9